Original title:
What Does Santa Do?

Copyright © 2024 Creative Arts Management OÜ
All rights reserved.

Author: Alexander Thornton
ISBN HARDBACK: 978-9916-90-844-0
ISBN PAPERBACK: 978-9916-90-845-7

A Map of Laughter and Light

In a sleigh that squeaks with cheer,
He charts a course for each dear soul.
With cookie crumbs and milk to steer,
He checks it twice, that's his role.

Rooftops acting like a slide,
He twirls and spins, oh what a sight!
The reindeer giggle, full of pride,
As they dash through the frosty night.

He wiggles down the chimneys tight,
With a bounce that rivals all the toys.
Spreading giggles, pure delight,
Creating chaos, oh what joys!

A wink for each child snug in bed,
Whispers of laughter fill the air.
Sneezes disguised, a pop of red,
He sneaks away without a care.

The Promise of December Nights

In frosty air, he makes his rounds,
With jingle bells that dance and chime.
Each laugh and cheer, a treasure found,
In snowflakes soft, a joy sublime.

His belly shakes like a bowl of jelly,
As he rides on through the starry glow.
With every laugh, he perks up belly,
For every home, he's sure to show.

He balances toys in a playful way,
Like juggling acts at the county fair.
With giggles echoing, night turns to day,
He tosses out surprises everywhere!

In every heart, he plants a seed,
Of laughter that blooms through the year.
With a wink and grin, he knows the need,
For joy to wrap us all in cheer.

Dreams Delivered in the Blink of an Eye

A flash of red crosses the sky,
With giggles trailing in his wake.
He whispers secrets, oh so sly,
As dreams take flight for all our sake.

Through frosted windows, he peeks in,
With Santa socks and funny hats.
A wink to signal where to begin,
With mischief, laughter, and playful spats.

The elves are busy, making noise,
While wrapping dreams in colorful sheets.
With Santa's glee, they share the joys,
Of holiday treats and sugary feats.

At dawn he's gone, but joy remains,
With every smile a story told.
In laughter bright as snowy plains,
The magic held within our fold.

Gifts Beyond Compare

In a sleigh that goes whoosh,
He slides down the flue,
With a grin so wide,
And a bag full of goo.

Elves dancing around,
With cocoa in hand,
They get slightly silly,
As they sing in a band.

Wrapping up giggles,
Each bow with a pop,
They tumble and giggle,
'Til they nearly flop.

With a mischievous wink,
He leaves quite a mess,
But joy in his wake,
Is the ultimate bless.

Once Upon a Christmas Eve

The stars light the sky,
With a twinkle and laugh,
Santa checks his list,
And splits it in half.

Reindeer leaping high,
On rooftops they prance,
While he slips down the chimney,
In a comical dance.

Cookies left out,
With milk in a cup,
Santa's loving feast,
Then the elves shake it up!

They hop and they spin,
To the rhythm of cheer,
Spreading joy through the night,
With a jolly good jeer.

The Rhythm of Ho-Ho-Ho

From the North with a cheer,
Comes a jolly old soul,
In red fuzzy pants,
With a belly like a bowl.

He chuckles along,
As he flies through the night,
With sleigh bells a-jingling,
What a glorious sight.

As he lands, what a clatter!
Elves dash left and right,
Santa starts with the giggles,
A most humorous sight.

He ho-ho-ho's loudly,
Tripping on a sock,
But with giggles and glee,
He puts it on his clock.

The Fabric of Magical Nights

In a world spun of dreams,
With whimsy and flair,
Santa stitches the night,
With a twinkle and care.

Through whispers of snow,
And laughter galore,
He threads in the magic,
That we all adore.

With a needle of joy,
He sews smiles so wide,
Each gift that he brings,
Is wrapped up with pride.

In the fabric of fun,
Every stitch holds delight,
As he weaves through the stars,
'Til the dawn turns to night.

Cherished Traditions in Flight

Reindeer prance with a shiny nose,
On rooftops high, they strike a pose.
With a twinkle and a dash, they zoom around,
Leaving surprises all over town.

In snowy nights, they take to the sky,
While warm milk waits and cookies lie.
They whisper secrets to the moon's bright glow,
Crafting tales of cheer as they go.

A sleigh full of laughter, it rolls and it sways,
As laughter drifts down through the snowy haze.
With a clap and a cheer, the magic unfolds,
In the heart of the night, all the wonders are told.

The Spirit Behind the Wrapping

Presents stacked with bows and flair,
Each one wrapped with utter care.
Tangles of ribbon, a sticky delight,
Unraveling giggles in the soft moonlight.

With tipsy tape and scissors that roam,
He crafts gifts far away from home.
Slapping on tags with names and glee,
Wondering who'll unwrap the spree.

Oh, the mischievous grin as he sneaks,
Feeling the joy in the laughter that peaks.
With every crinkle, excitement is born,
In the cozy embrace of a magical morn.

Nightly Visits and Silent Wishes

From chimney tops, he slides with flair,
Tiptoeing softly, with utmost care.
He checks his list for the nice and the naughty,
Chuckling at stories, both sweet and haughty.

In the heart of the night, he whispers a cheer,
While toys and giggles spread far and near.
Silent wishes float like snowflakes around,
Crafting joy in the softest sound.

As stockings swell with secrets untold,
He nibbles snacks and feels quite bold.
With a wink and a wave, he's off in a flash,
Leaving memories to cherish and clash.

Joyful Labor of Love

With a belly that shakes like a bowl full of jelly,
He dances and laughs, oh so merry and smelly!
Churning out toys with a wink and a grin,
Making magic with every spin!

Elves scamper about with a flourish and flair,
Crafting joy with exceptional care.
In the workshop they bubble, they giggle, they sing,
Creating enchantments that each child will bring.

A joyful labor, oh what a sight,
Sparkling eyes in the magical night.
Together they cherish the spirit of play,
As they spread holiday cheer in every way!

Navigating the Winter Sky

Up in the air with a map on his knee,
Santa's lost track of where he should be.
With a wink and a grin, he swerves through the snow,
Avoiding the clouds that are blocking his glow.

In a sleigh made of candy and reindeer delight,
He twirls through the stars, what a comical sight!
With a chuckle so loud, he adjusts his old hat,
"Which way to the cookies?" he giggles and chats.

Sprinkles of Magic

Elves in the workshop are up to some tricks,
Mixing up potions with sprinkles and kicks.
One stirs a cauldron while dancing a jig,
Another is juggling a very big gig!

With a sprinkle of laughter, they giggle with glee,
"Let's make some gifts for the kids and for me!"
With rainbows and sparkles, they giggle and cheer,
Creating a whirlwind of holiday cheer.

Songs from the Elves

Elves gather 'round, with a banjo and drum,
Singing the praises of holiday fun.
Their voices are silly, the tunes really bright,
Caroling jokes that cause Santa to bite.

Each verse is a giggle, a pun or a rhyme,
Laughter erupts, oh, it's jolly good time!
With a wink and a nod, they dance on their toes,
"We'll sing through the night, until Santa just dozes!"

Reindeer Games Under the Stars

Under the stars, reindeer prance and play,
With antlers that twinkle, they light up the way.
Donner has hiccups; it's causing a fuss,
While Blitzen keeps bouncing and giving a thrust.

Prancing in circles, it's a four-legged race,
Each one trying hard to keep up the pace.
With snowflakes flying, they tumble and roll,
"Who knew that this night could be so out of control?"

Sparkling Memories of Childhood

On snowy nights, with cookies laid,
A chubby man, in red, displayed.
He'd nibble, sip, and laugh with glee,
While reindeer danced upon my tree.

The gifts piled high, one by one,
With tags that teased, oh what fun!
I'd peek and giggle, eyes all wide,
As magic sleighs took joyful ride.

Santa's belt, it stretched so tight,
He'd wiggle down, a comical sight.
And in my dreams, he'd share a grin,
With twinkling eyes, let the games begin.

Oh, memories bright, those carefree hours,
With playful moments and cookie powers.
The laughter echoes, still so clear,
Of Santa's antics, year to year.

The Joyful Journey to Every Home

Rooftops high, he takes a leap,
While children giggle, not a peep.
Down chimneys quick, but oh so sly,
With jolly squeals, 'Tis time to fly!

In every nook, he leaves a prize,
With playful tricks that break all ties.
A sprinkle here, a wink right there,
He fills the night with festive flair.

On frosty paths, his sleigh takes flight,
With cookies tossed, oh what a sight!
Each house adorned with lights aglow,
As Santa cheers, ho ho ho!

The joyous ride, a merry chase,
With laughter lining every space.
He knows each child, each gift to bring,
A comic tale, in winter's swing.

Merry Secrets of the Moonlight

In moonlit shadows, secrets fly,
A jolly figure, catching my eye.
He whispers tales, all wrapped in cheer,
While tiptoeing close, I hardly hear.

With giggles muffled, I watch him sway,
As he juggles gifts in a playful way.
Each shimmered bow, a rascally clue,
Of mischief planned, and fun to ensue.

His laughter echoes through the night,
With twinkling stars, a splendid sight.
The moon grins down, not wanting to miss,
This nightly caper filled with bliss.

With surprise-filled packages to unfold,
He dances like he's three years old.
Oh, those secrets shared without a care,
In the moonlight, joy is everywhere.

The Countdown to Cheer

The calendar flips, the days tick by,
Anticipation makes spirits fly.
Each door we open, joy unconfined,
As Santa plots, with laughter entwined.

The countdown's fun, with glitter and glue,
Crafting garlands, red and blue.
He peeks on us, from far away,
With cheeky sparkles to save the day.

In jingle bells, he hides a clue,
A riddle that's silly for me and you.
With every giggle, he stirs the stew,
Of memories made, both old and new.

So here's to cheer, a festive toast,
To Santa's antics we love the most.
In every heart, his laughter stays,
As we count down to those merry days.

Choreography of Cheer

Dancing with reindeer in the snow,
Twinkling lights put on quite a show.
He juggles gifts with a wink and a smile,
Keeping the elves entertained all the while.

Cookies and milk as a secret snack,
Trying to hide from the elf's sly track.
With a belly that jiggles, he takes a break,
Planning his moves for the big night's stake.

Falling down chimneys, oh what a sight,
Contorting like acrobats in the night.
Spreading joy with a flip and a twist,
Leaving a trail that cannot be missed.

Laughter erupts as he slides down fast,
A comedic routine that's unsurpassed.
Wrapped in red with a sleigh full of cheer,
He's the star performer of the year!

Santa's Secret Agenda

Sipping hot cocoa, he plots his spree,
Finding the best route, like a mystery.
Checking the lists, he skips on one toe,
Deciding who's naughty and who's a pro.

His smartphone buzzing with holiday cheer,
Texting the elves that the party is near.
"Santa's on duty, so keep up the pace!"
With a wink and a grin, he puts on his face.

Elves in the workshop start a surprise,
Building up gadgets that light up the skies.
Whispering secrets behind closed doors,
"Big guy's got tricks; what're we waiting for?"

With red velvet plans and a cheeky cheer,
He's orchestrating fun year after year.
From rooftops he jumps, in a blur he appears,
His secret agenda brings laughter and cheers!

The Gift of Giving

He wraps up each present with ribbons and flair,
Tossing in giggles and love in the air.
Every gift given is a chance to delight,
Bringing pancakes on Christmas Eve night.

Bouncing on rooftops, he's light as a feather,
Throwing surprises that bring folks together.
From bicycles to dolls, all wonders abound,
A sprinkling of magic on joyful ground.

He sneezes while wrapping, oh what a sight,
Papers and bows taking off in flight.
With glimmers of glee, he spreads his pure joy,
Santa's delight — the ultimate ploy!

Through the frosty air, he bumbles and beams,
Dancing and sliding, lost in his dreams.
The gift of giving's his favorite cheer,
With laughter and love, he fills up the year!

Sleigh Bells and Silent Nights

Sleigh bells jingle as he takes to the skies,
Hovering over rooftops, he laughs and he sighs.
Mischief in the air, he twirls with delight,
Landing at houses in the still of the night.

With a snicker and chuckle, he sneaks through the door,
Leaving a trail of whipped cream on the floor.
Caught in the act by a sleepy-eyed child,
"Did you see me dance? I'm so free and wild!"

Snowflakes dance lightly as he makes his retreat,
Sleigh full of giggles and treats to complete.
In silent nights, he's the jester of cheer,
Tickling the fancies of all who are near.

With twinkling lights and a grin full of glee,
He's the life of the party for all to see.
In this joyful season, he spins round and round,
Sleigh bells and laughter, the best joy we've found!

The Spirit of Giving

Elves are busy, all day long,
Packing socks, singing their song.
Rudolph's nose is shining bright,
Guiding sleighs through the night.

Cookies piled, oh what a sight!
Sugar rush, a pure delight.
Santa's on his jolly route,
With a belly that's round and stout.

Jingle bells, laughter all around,
As reindeer prance upon the ground.
Gifts and giggles, oh so grand,
In every house across the land.

In the Heart of Winter

Snowflakes dance with twinkling cheer,
While Santa's stuck in a spinning sphere.
With a wink and a jolly laugh,
He tripped on a toy's silly giraffe.

The Frosty Friends play tag with glee,
While snowmen wish to sip hot tea.
Santa's sleigh is stuck in snow!
But he's giggling, 'Oh ho ho!'

Bundled up against the cold,
His merry spirit never old.
Elfin laughter fills the air,
'This is fun!' they cry, without a care.

Twilight in Toyland

Dolls are dancing, on their toes,
While robots whirr and strike a pose.
In Toyland's twilight, magic roams,
As teddy bears claim cozy homes.

Santa's checking, oh what a thrill,
'Is that a bike or just a grill?'
Elves giggle behind toy trees,
'They'll be puzzled!' they shout with glee!

Magic sparkles fill the air,
As laughter flows without a care.
Santa winks, it's all in fun,
When crafting mischief has begun!

Workshop of Wonders

In the workshop, tools are flying,
As Santa watches, slowly sighing.
'Is that a bike or a circus clown?'
Elves just chuckle; they won't frown.

Amidst the chaos and the cheer,
Santa's searching for his reindeer.
Toy trains zoom; a doll takes flight,
'Oops,' says Santa, 'That's not right!'

Chipping wood and painting bright,
Elves work hard into the night.
'What will they think of next?' he muses,
As laughter flows and joy confuses.

Chocolate Dreams and Reindeer Schemes

In a factory filled with bliss,
Elves craft treats you can't resist.
Chocolate rivers flow and swirl,
While reindeer dance and twirl.

Sugar sprinkles in the air,
Joyful laughter everywhere.
Santa's belly, round and tight,
Jumps on scales, oh what a sight!

Cookies stacked up to the sky,
Reindeer munching, oh my, oh my!
Mapping routes through frosty skies,
Naughty lists, those little lies.

With a wink and twinkling eye,
Santa flies and shouts a "Hi!"
Toy trains whistle, sleds all gleam,
In this land of chocolate dreams.

Whispers of Starlit Snow

On rooftops, soft whispers fall,
Tiny feet, both quick and small.
Elves in snowmen hats parade,
Laughing, giggling, and they played.

With a twirl, and a shout,
Sleigh bells ringing all about.
Underneath the starlit glow,
Gifts appear, oh how they flow!

Reindeer prance in perfect rows,
Whiskers twitch and laughter grows.
Santa's sleigh, a sight to see,
Zipping by so endlessly!

Snowflakes dance as giggles soar,
Elves shout out, "Let's make more!"
In this land where dreams are sown,
Joyous whispers, softly blown.

The Elves' Countdown to Cheer

Ticking clocks with jingle sounds,
Elves are racing all around.
Wrapping paper, bows galore,
Each surprises ties up more!

One, two, three, the countdown near,
Chests filled up with fun and cheer.
Giggles bubbling in the air,
Spreading joy with sparkles rare!

Santa's list, a tangled mess,
"Oops! We forgot the red dress!"
With a wink, they grab some glue,
"What a sight! Look! It's shiny too!"

Counting down with sneaky grins,
Mimicking the reindeer spins.
In their hearts, good cheer will brew,
As Christmas magic's born anew.

Ho Ho Home for the Holidays

Santa's sleigh with cushions bright,
Rides the stars, oh what a sight!
Ho ho ho, he shouts with glee,
Landing softly by the tree.

Cookies baked with love and charm,
Santa eats without alarm!
Milk awaits with mucho flair,
Slurping loud, then "C'mon! Share!"

Reindeer kick with festive cheer,
Prancing 'round, they spread good cheer.
Time for fun and counting joys,
Laughing loud with all the toys!

Now he's home, in comfy seat,
Santa dreams of sugary treats.
While the snowflakes dance and play,
Joyful hearts will lead the way.

The Reindeer's Dance

In the moonlight, they prance with glee,
Shaking their tails, wild and free.
Hooves tap the snow, a jingling sound,
Dancing in circles, they spin all around.

With a shake of their antlers, they twirl, oh so bright,
Making the stars laugh in the night.
Around the North Pole, they stomp and shout,
Crafting a party without a doubt!

They play with the elves, in a joyful spree,
Tossing snowballs like it's a jubilee.
These lively friends, full of zest and cheer,
Make the days merry as Christmas draws near.

Their frolicking footsteps, a sight to behold,
With giggles and howls, a story retold.
Each twist and turn, like a winter's ballet,
Leaving behind a trail, come what may.

Snowflakes and Sweet Treats

Frosty treats good enough to eat,
Covered in sugar, oh, what a feat!
Snowflakes dance down, all sparkly and bright,
Landing on cookies, a cozy delight.

Marshmallow snowmen, adorned with a grin,
Ready for nibbling, let the fun begin!
Chocolate rivers flow, rich and divine,
Candy cane trails, a sugary line.

The elves roll the dough, with laughter so loud,
Shaping new goodies for every proud crowd.
Popped popcorn like snow, fluffy and white,
Sledding on trays, what a magical sight!

With giggles and grins, the kitchens are bright,
Creating sweet joys that feel just right.
A sprinkle of fun, a scoop of delight,
Snowflakes and sweetness, oh, what a night!

The Art of Delight

Crafty hands work with ribbons and flair,
Gifts of all sizes are made with care.
Laughter erupts as the paper takes flight,
Twirling and swirling, such a colorful sight.

Elves hum a tune, like bees in a hive,
Each package they wrap, it comes alive!
Glitter and bows all dance in the air,
Creating surprises beyond compare.

The art of delight is a messy affair,
With sticky fingers and stories to share.
They giggle and wiggle, a whimsical crew,
Turning the workshop into a zoo!

With magic in each fold, and giggles in tow,
Wrapping up joy in this sweet, festive show.
Come light up the night, with laughter so bright,
As art comes alive, bringing pure delight!

A Night with the Merry Makers

Gather 'round, it's the latest trend,
Holiday cheer is around the bend.
The merry makers shout and cheer,
Bringing together all those held dear.

Games and giggles end up in a race,
Who can slide fastest, what a wild chase!
Bouncing and bouncing, like popcorn in air,
The fun never stops; Oh, forget all your care!

Mug of hot cocoa, marshmallows afloat,
Tales of old antics written by rote.
A chorus of laughter spills out in waves,
As silly antics end up like braves.

With a wink and a nod, they play through the night,
Under the stars, what a marvelous sight!
In the warmth of goodwill and cheer that they bring,
A night with the merry makers gives hearts wings!

The Mystique of Merry Delights

In the night, he checks his list,
With a wink and a little twist.
Searching for every good surprise,
Are socks or toys the bigger prize?

His reindeer prance on roofs so high,
Belly full, he lets out a sigh.
Cookies gone, just crumbs remain,
While he giggles on the windowpane.

Riding sleighs through thick, white fluff,
He makes toys, just never enough.
With a jolly laugh, he gives a cheer,
What's he scheming? Only he's clear!

As dawn breaks with morning light,
Santa's off, he's out of sight.
But whispers tell of his big plans,
With candy canes and merry fans.

Legends of the St. Nick's Lane

In the shop, toys dance and gleam,
Santa's there, or so we dream.
With elf assistants on the go,
Bouncing around, we're in for a show!

With a belly that shakes like a bowl,
Every gift comes from the heart and soul.
Naughty or nice, he just can't tell,
When the elves slip him cookies—oh, what a spell!

He rides his sleigh at the strike of night,
With speedy reindeer and sheer delight.
Swapping secrets with the moon's glow,
Sneaking peeks at the world below.

At the end, he gives a shout,
"Let's head home, there's fun, no doubt!"
Through laughter and cheer, the night wraps tight,
With kangaroos in jammies, quite a sight!

Frosty Whispers from the Past

In December's chill, tales are spun,
Of Santa's antics—oh, what fun!
Building snowmen, dodging snowballs,
He giggles as his sleigh lightly falls.

A hat on his head, boots so bright,
He slides down chimneys with pure delight.
Leaving gifts, some wrapped in haste,
He often fears he'll run out of space!

With every laugh, a wish made true,
Santa wears red, that much we knew.
But could it be that he's a clown,
When he trips and tumbles down the town?

Yet with love in each present he brings,
He dances 'round, twirling strings.
So as the night fades, we all share,
His merry mishap becomes our care!

Under Wraps and Overjoyed

In a corner, Santa counts his loot,
Beside him is a big red boot.
Wrapped surprises stacked around,
Peeking inside, what joy is found!

Jingle bells make quite the sound,
As he stirs mayhem all around.
With reindeer games and silly pranks,
He snickers softly as the fire flanks.

He gets caught on a sticky chair,
Can't reach cookies? He's got flair!
With ribbons tangled in his beard,
"Oh dear!" he laughs, "Where is my beard?"

Under wraps, the night proceeds,
Filled with giggles and silly deeds.
Santa's joy is all we need,
With funny tales of Christmas speed!

North Pole Adventures

Santa's sleigh with reindeer flies,
Through frosty air and snowy skies.
Elves dance on the workshop floor,
Jingle bells, they shout for more!

With mittens warm and cocoa hot,
They build the toys, each tiny bot.
But who slipped on that shiny floor?
An elf flew high and hit the door!

Santa checks his giant list,
Frowning hard, oh what a twist!
Who's been naughty? Who's been nice?
Oh dear, now that would suffice!

With all the giggles and some whirls,
They paint the sleds in glittered swirls.
Laughter echoes, a joyful sound,
In the North Pole, fun's always found!

The Sounds of the Season

Hear the jingles, bells a-ringing,
Santa's voice, cheerfully singing.
Elves making toys with giggles bright,
In the snowy day and starry night.

A crash! Oh no! What was that noise?
Santa slipped while checking toys.
Elves burst out in laughter and cheer,
"Don't worry, folks, he's still right here!"

The sound of laughter fills the air,
While snowflakes dance, without a care.
Santa's sled, so full and bright,
Zooms through the sky, a lovely sight!

With candy canes and hearty laughs,
They share the joy, they share the crafts.
In this jolly, merry town,
Smiles are worn, never a frown!

Sleds and Sweet Dreams

Underneath the twinkling stars,
Santa's testing out his cars.
With a whoosh and a zip so fast,
He zips and zooms, oh what a blast!

Elves on sleds fly down the hill,
Laughing loud, they've got the thrill.
But one small elf, named Timmy T,
Fell in a pile of powdered tree!

Sweet dreams are made of cookie dough,
While reindeer munch on mistletoe.
Santa grins with a twinkle bright,
"Time for all to rest tonight!"

With pillows fluffed and blankets snug,
He whispers softly, gives a hug.
In dreams, they ride the skies so far,
With laughter ringing, just like a star!

Unwrapping Wishes

Presents piled as high as trees,
Santa's busy, bustling with glee.
With every ribbon and shiny bow,
A surprise awaits, oh don't you know?

Elves gather 'round with a cheer,
"Let's unbox joy! The time is here!"
But be careful of that fragile thing,
Oops! That was Timmy's favorite spring!

With wrappings torn and laughter loud,
Santa stands tall, so overflowing proud.
"Each gift is magic, a wish to make,
Let's share the joy, for goodness sake!"

As the moon casts a silvery glow,
They pile the gifts in a joyful row.
Wishes floating on the chilly breeze,
In this season, our hearts are at ease!

Glimmering Wrappings

He juggles gifts, oh what a sight,
With ribbons tangled, oh so tight.
Elves are giggling, it's quite the show,
As paper flies and bows will go.

He sneaks in cookies, leaving crumbs,
While reindeer prance, making fun sounds.
With every roar and joyful cheer,
He dances 'round, spreading delight here.

Bright lights twinkle as he takes flight,
Through chimney tops, he's out of sight.
A lollipop stuck to the roof he found,
Licking away while spinning 'round.

Down goes Santa, what a big thud!
Covered in soot, a jolly old stud.
With laughter echoing through the night,
He wiggles his nose, what a goofy sight!

A Sleigh Ride into Tomorrow

Off he goes with a dash and a zoom,
Over rooftops and into the gloom.
A sleigh filled high, it's quite the load,
Elves in the back, more tricks they've showed.

With cookies galore, they munch and play,
As Santa steers, they shout hooray!
The stars are buzzing, what a delight,
In a sleigh ride swirling the frosty night.

A twist and a twirl while speeding through air,
Santa hopes he hasn't lost a pair.
The bells are jingling, what a loud din,
Crazy reindeer, let the games begin!

Tomorrow's gifts, all piled so high,
Moments of laughter, oh me, oh my!
With a wink and a nod, they'll zoom with glee,
Adventure awaits, just wait and see!

Enchanted Nights of Giving

He tiptoes softly, can you believe,
Perfectly quiet, like a thief on leave.
Gifts in hand, he shuffles around,
On enchanted nights, joy knows no bounds.

With a whoosh and a woosh, he'll disappear,
Leaving behind filled hearts and good cheer.
Stockings await, what treasures inside?
Adventure and laughter, oh what a ride!

He's stuck in a chimney, just a bit wide,
Squeezing and slipping with nowhere to hide.
The elves are cackling, oh what a sight,
As they fish him out for his merry flight!

Giggles abound in the starry sky,
As he cheerfully waves, "Oh my, oh my!"
With that jolly belly and rosy red nose,
Santa leaves chuckles wherever he goes!

Holiday Whispers in the Wind

Late in the night, he lets out a laugh,
Stirring the snow and the reindeer staff.
While dancing shadows leap across the ground,
Holiday whispers fill the air around.

He picks up the pace, with a hop and a skip,
Dancing with joy, what a jolly trip!
The stars are winking as he glides true,
With a bag full of giggles, just for you.

In every house he spreads such charm,
Avoids the black cats, arms out to disarm.
He flips a coin, what a festive spin,
With each jolly blessing, let the fun begin!

As dawn draws near, he lets out a cheer,
The night's escapades now perfectly clear.
With a tip of his hat and a wink in his eye,
He zooms up the sky, oh my, oh my!

Beyond the Northern Lights

Jolly old guy on a sleigh,
Spinning around in a merry ballet.
He checks his list, makes some notes,
While dancing with reindeer on fluffy coats.

With cookies and milk, he fuels his flight,
Dancing with elves in the shimmering night.
Spreading cheer with a giggle and grin,
Hidden in snowflakes, where the fun begins.

In the crisp air, he whispers a joke,
Snickering softly, he can't help but choke.
His belly shakes like a bowl full of jelly,
As he tumbles down chimneys, oh what a telly!

A sleigh full of giggles, a sack of delight,
Shooting stars dance, a whimsical sight.
Beyond the lights where merriment roams,
He's the king of the night, in his laughter, we hone.

The Magic of St. Nick

When Santa rolls out in his big red suit,
He juggles oranges, oh what a hoot!
Twirling and whirling, he makes quite the scene,
With candy canes launched like a festive machine.

His eyes twinkle bright with a cheeky glow,
He's known to indulge in a dance with the snow.
Swooshing and sliding, he twirls with delight,
Leaving giggles behind on this magical night.

With a wink and a nod, he promises cheer,
Sharing laughter and joy, bringing everyone near.
Waving to children, he makes a grand show,
Munching on treats as he dashes below.

So if you catch sight of a twinkle up high,
Know that old St. Nick is ever so spry.
With a chuckle and cheer, he spreads the fun,
Enchanting the world 'til the night is done.

Christmas Constellations

In a sky full of twinkles, Santa takes flight,
Singing to stars on a frosty night.
With laughter so loud it could wake the moon,
His reindeer hum tunes that make hearts swoon.

Galaxies giggle as they dance in the dark,
Santa joins in, his jigs leave a mark.
He spins among planets and hops past a star,
Grabbing stardust from his sleigh, oh so far!

Winking at comets, they zip by his side,
While planets all cheer, oh what a ride!
With each little laugh, he crafts a new tale,
In a universe bright, where joys never pale.

So look up and see, when the Christmas lights glow,
Santa's up there making magic flow.
In the constellations, he leaves his fun trace,
In the heart of the night, he finds his place.

Gifts Wrapped in Hope

In a workshop so bright, where the laughter won't cease,
Santa's wrapping up joy with a sprinkle of peace.
Each gift has a giggle, a jingle, a spark,
Tied neatly with ribbons, shiny and stark.

The elves are a whirlwind, with tape in their hands,
Building new toys, following Santa's grand plans.
They slip on banana peels, laughter abounds,
Creating the quirkiest, silliest sounds.

With a dash of confetti and sprinkles of cheer,
Santa shimmies around as the holiday nears.
He tosses out wishes like candy from dreams,
In a flurry of giggles, or so it seems!

After all the hustle, the twinkles are bright,
Each gift carries hope, spreading love into night.
With a chuckle and cheer, this is the score,
Gifts wrapped in hope, joy forevermore!

Guiding Lights of December

Under a moon that's bright and round,
Reindeer prance without a sound.
Santa checks his list with glee,
Is this the best gift for me?

Cookies crumble as he takes a bite,
Milk mustaches bring delight.
With jingles and chuckles in the air,
He dances 'round without a care.

His sleigh is parked on the roof,
He scoffs at GPS, oh what a goof!
While elves play tricks behind his back,
He's blissfully lost in a holiday snack.

But as dawn breaks, gifts all around,
Laughter and joy in every sound.
Off he goes, with a wink and a cheer,
Next year he'll return, never fear!

Cherished Moments in Time

Upon the shelf, the snowmen grin,
As Santa sneaks, just to get in.
With a belly laugh, he spins around,
Creating chaos, gift-giving bound.

Elves play pranks, not making toys,
Instead, spreading glittery joys.
A hat on a cat, a scarf on the dog,
All in the spirit, like a holiday fog.

He shimmy-shakes, he giggles, he glides,
Clumsily stuck in chimneys, he hides.
With a tinkle of bells, joy fills the air,
As he slips on his sleigh with a comedic flair.

In homes aglow, the laughter rings,
Santa's antics: oh, the joy it brings!
And though he's jolly with a sly little wink,
He's also just here for the cookies and drink!

Mysteries of the Workshop

In a workshop buzzing, oh what a sight,
Elves in a frenzy from morning to night.
Toys flying off the assembly line,
Do they know they're gifts or just divine?

Amidst the laughter and playful shouts,
There's always someone breaking out doubts.
"Where's that robot?" one elf will squeal,
"Oh no! He's dancing on the big wheel!"

Sawdust rainbows fill the room,
No time for gloom, just festive boom!
In each corner, a mischief unfold,
Cramming in giggles, if you're bold.

Machines whirr in a chaotic tune,
As toys find their bows under the moon.
Santa peeks in—what's his delight?
It's just another dance-off, oh what a night!

The Warmth of Holiday Spirits

By the fireside, hot cocoa flows,
Santa warms up while the wind blows.
With a grin so wide and a chuckle so deep,
He's lost in stories that never sleep.

Jingle bells ring as he tells a tale,
Of reindeer pranks that never fail.
Stuck in a tree, oh what a sight,
His laughter echoes through the chilly night.

Sprinkled with cheer, the magic scarf glows,
Warming up children from heads to toes.
As socks get hung with a playful flair,
Santa shrinks down, just to share.

With joy in his heart and mischief afoot,
He hugs the cookies—and the cat, to boot!
For amidst the warmth of laughter and song,
Santa's spirit leads us all along.

The Keeper of Holiday Cheer

In a sleigh with a jingling sound,
He's bringing joy all around.
Elves giggle, they dance and sing,
While he checks if you've been a good thing.

With a belly that shakes like a bowl of jelly,
He munches on snacks, quite the merry medley.
Throwing snowballs from rooftops high,
His laughter echoes, oh my, oh my!

Putting gifts in a sack, quite the task,
Mischief's his game, no need to ask.
He sneaks past the cat, oh so sly,
Leaving presents, oh what a guy!

When kids are dreaming, he's on the roam,
Turning rooftops into his home.
With a wink and a grin, he takes flight,
Spreading happiness under the moonlight.

Journeying Through the Frost

Through the snowflakes, he makes his way,
With a twinkling smile, he loves to play.
Reindeer prance on rooftops high,
While stars twinkle brightly in the sky.

What's that sound? A clatter and shuffle,
He dodges the snowmen, a playful scuffle.
His cheeks rosy from cold and glee,
Munching on gingerbread, oh can't you see?

With a list that's too long to keep,
He finds time for fun before children sleep.
Catching snowflakes, he twirls around,
Creating laughter, that joyful sound!

Twirling in circles, he slips and slides,
In and out of chimneys, oh how he glides!
His heart full of cheer, and maybe some pie,
Journeying far, oh my, oh my!

Threads of Milk and Cookies

A plate laid out with sweets galore,
He sneaks a nibble, then some more.
Milk in a glass sits waiting there,
He twirls like a dancer, oh what flair!

Cookies crumbling, a delightful mess,
With frosting on his beard, he's in a stress.
'Just one more bite!' he says with a grin,
While elves giggle, oh what a win!

He rates the snacks with a playful sigh,
'Not too burnt, oh, oh my, oh my!'
Each year he swears to eat just a few,
But the treats are too tempting, oh how they woo!

His sack's overflowing, gifts bringing cheer,
Yet cookies and milk still disappear.
Leaving laughter and crumbs for the next day,
In a cozy home, he'll merrily stay.

The Yule Log's Glow

By the crackling fire, warmth fills the room,
Stories unfold, dispelling the gloom.
He giggles and snickers, sharing a tale,
While marshmallows roast, getting fluffy and pale.

With a flick of his wrist, he sparks up the light,
Filling the air with a magical sight.
Cookies sprout legs, they dance around,
While he chuckles at joy that is found.

From the mantle hangs stockings, all in a row,
He bestows silly gifts, such a great show!
With a wink and a hop, he brings cheer,
Singing songs that everyone can hear.

As the Yule log burns bright, stories unwind,
He spreads laughter and love, oh so kind.
Belly shaking with joy, wrapped in delight,
Celebrating the season, all through the night.

The Midnight Craftsman

In the hush of night, when all is still,
Santa's off to work with a jolly thrill.
He tinkers and toils, with a gleeful shout,
Making toys and gadgets, with giggles throughout.

The reindeer peek in, eyes all aglow,
Wondering what antics the old man will show.
With a plucky little elf dancing on the floor,
He's hiding behind the toolbox, laughing for more.

The workshop buzzes, tools clank and clatter,
Each toy a mystery, what's this? A splatter!
He slips on a wrench—oh what a sight!
Spinning like a top, oh what a delight!

So if you hear laughter as you drift off to sleep,
It's Santa and pals, not promises to keep.
With a wink and a grin, ready for the ride,
Crafting each toy, with magic as his guide.

Sleigh Bells and Stardust

Under the moonlight, with sleigh bells ringing,
Santa juggles gifts, laughing and singing.
He trips over carrots, the reindeer snort,
But with a hearty laugh, he'll never fall short.

With stardust sprinkled, the night's full of cheer,
He dances on rooftops, spreading good cheer.
Ho ho ho! He chuckles, sliding down fast,
Dodging all chimneys—oh what a blast!

The sleigh zips along, through the shimmering night,
Gifts bouncing about, oh what a sight!
Packed with surprises, oh dear, what's this?
An army of toys? It can't be amiss!

With giggles and guffaws, he spreads holiday love,
A mischievous wink from the skies up above.
Sleigh bells keep ringing, all through the air,
As Santa zooms past with a jolly old flair.

Whispering Wishes

In the quiet of dreams, as the children all sleep,
Santa whispers secrets, for the magic to keep.
With a twinkle in his eye, he crafts with care,
Every little wish, floating up in the air.

He pulls out a ribbon, a roll of bright tape,
Creating a whole world, oh what a shape!
Transforming plain boxes with laughter and fun,
Each little surprise, a race to be won.

The stockings all bulge, stuffed full with delight,
As Santa sneaks in on this magical night.
He giggles a tune, with a tip of his hat,
For it's not just the gifts—it's the joy of the chat!

So come Christmas morning, with eyes open wide,
They'll find all his magic, right there by their side.
A jolly adventure, wrapped up with a smile,
The sweetest of whispers will make it worthwhile.

The Elves' Secret Workshop

Deep in the forest, where mischief brews,
The elves cheer him on, with plenty of cues.
Poking and prodding, they work in a rush,
Building new gadgets in a frenzy and hush.

With tools all laid out, and coffee in hand,
They scheme and they dream, making toys so grand.
But wait, what's that? An elf slips and trips!
Into a pile of plushies, he flips and he flips!

Santa gives orders, with a laugh and a grin,
"Don't worry, my friends, let the fun begin!"
A squeaky toy here, a doll with a hat,
In this busy workshop, there's never a spat.

As the clock ticks down, they hurry with glee,
For delivering joy is as fun as can be.
With a wink and a nudge, ready for the flight,
The elves and Santa! What a hilarious sight!

A Journey Through Snow

In a sleigh big and bright, he takes flight,
With reindeer who giggle, a comical sight.
They dash through the night, all bundled and warm,
Spreading joy and odd gifts in a crazy charm.

Around every bend, they honk and they glide,
Missing the chimney? Well, that's just their pride!
Down the wrong flue, they stumble and crash,
Leaving behind a cacophony and clash.

Snowflakes dance 'round as they take a sharp turn,
Gifts tumble and roll, for giggles they yearn.
With a wink and a grin, they just laugh it away,
For what's a few mix-ups on this crazy sleigh day?

Through winters so wild, they make quite the fuss,
Spreading laughter and joy, do we dare to discuss?
In the end, every gift leads to giggles anew,
Who knew snowflakes could lead to such joy a few?

The Legacy of Laughter

He sneaks in the night with a chuckle and cheer,
His bag clinks and clatters, oh, what will appear?
A rubber chicken? A popper? Nothing's too wild,
For Santa's a jester, a batty old child.

He jingles his bells, not just for the show,
But to tickle the funny bones, don't you know?
In a tower of toys, he finds quite the mix,
With a whoopee cushion and seltzer for kicks.

His laugh echoes loud as he tiptoes on floors,
While kids snicker softly behind bedroom doors.
They know that their stocking's not filled just with socks,

But gags, goofs, and giggles — it's creative flocks!

Oh, the joy that he brings, with his quirky flair,
With elves in the ranks, making mischief to share.
Every year, the legend of laughter, it thrives,
With Santa the silly, who keeps joy alive!

Midnight Deliveries

Under the moon, with a jingle and jive,
Santa speeds forth, oh, how he does thrive!
But oops! That's a mix-up, this giant brown sack,
Contains some new fur coats, not toys in the pack.

He lands on a roof, with a hop and a skip,
Falls right on the chimney, and does a quick flip!
A tumble of laughter, as he hollers, "Oh dear!"
While the reindeer below are all roaring with cheer.

He wiggles and jiggles, slipping down with grace,
Finds pudding and pies left just in one place.
"A snack for the road!" he grins with delight,
As crumbs scatter 'round in the glow of moonlight.

With each house he visits, there's always a laugh,
As he mixes up gifts — that's just Santa's path!
But at break of dawn, when children awake,
They'll giggle at gifts, oh, the mess that he makes!

Route of the Reindeer

On a route that's absurd, those reindeer take flight,
With a loop and a twist, they're a comical sight.
They duck and they dive, just to give you a grin,
Doing flips and some tricks, oh, where to begin?

They zigzag through clouds, with Santa in tow,
A dance through the air, with a twirl and a bow.
"Oops! That's a tree!" one shouts with a laugh,
As they bounce off it lightly, steering off path!

With each house they hit, there's a peculiar cheer,
A hula hoop here, and a crazy new deer.
They giggle and chime, sharing jokes up on high,
While Santa just grins, with a twinkle in his eye.

At last, they return to the North Pole so bright,
Exchanging loud tales of their flight in the night.
For the journey was silly, a riot, a blast,
As they settle in snug, thankful for the past!

Dusting Off the Red Suit

He pulled it from the closet, and gave a sneeze,
The suit was dusty, covered in cheese.
He checked the pockets for candy and toys,
And found a few notes from his old, noisy boys.

He wiggled and jiggled, it fit just right,
With pants that could stretch for a candy bite.
The bells on his shoes jingled a laugh,
He almost tripped over his holiday staff.

With a chuckle and grin, he looked in the mirror,
His jacket was red, but his belly was clear.
"I need to lose weight, or buy bigger pants!"
He pranced and he danced like he thought he could
chance.

So off to the fridge for a cookie or two,
"Then after some milk, I'll be good as new!"
His laughter echoed through the chilly night,
As he gets ready for his big festive flight.

Reindeer Games and Holiday Frames

The reindeer were gathered, all snug in a row,
Playing poker with snowflakes and glittering glow.
Rudolph dealt cards with a wink and a wink,
While Dasher and Dancer poured out the drink.

They argued and laughed over who'd take the lead,
"Not me! I'm still mad about last year's speed!"
"But your nose is so bright, you guide the way!"
"Only when sleepy, I snore all day!"

Up came the jingle from a curious elf,
"Boys, can you focus? We need Santa's help!"
They paused their game, with a big rolling cheer,
"Let's help him out, we got time till next year!"

So off they took off, balloons in a string,
Making snow angels—the reindeer could swing!
With laughter and giggles, they'd fly through the skies,
Delivering joy, to everyone's surprise!

The Heartbeat of December

In a little workshop, the clocks all ticked,
While Santa hummed tunes as the elves all clicked.
With gadgets and gizmos all scattered around,
He brewed hot cocoa while jolly bells sound.

Amidst all the chaos, a soft tune played,
Couples would dance, while the young ones paraded.
The rhythm of joy pulsed loud through the night,
As cozy warmth spread, 'neath the soft starlight.

With laughter and cheer echoing through the air,
He wrapped up each present with style and flair.
A mixtape of giggles spun 'round every gift,
While stockings got hung with a whimsical lift.

So in December, as snowflakes swirl high,
You'll find Santa's heartbeat, as sweet as a pie.
While he works and he plays, with a smile so grand,
Creating the magic, with a twinkling hand.

A Letter to the North Star

Dear North Star, I hope you're shining bright,
I'm writing to you on this chilly night.
The elves sent me questions, all silly and bold,
Like, "Are we too young to help if we're old?"

The workshop's alive, with no shortage of cheer,
But can you remind them to keep their hands clear?
Last week they flew over the candy cane trees,
And almost got stuck in a box of baked peas!

Oh, how they giggle and cackle away,
Trying to catch snowflakes while eating some hay.
So if you're still starlight, with your shimmering spark,
Shoot down a reminder—they're missing the mark!

As I wrap up this letter and sip my hot brew,
I wish you could hear all the jokes we now do.
So spark up the heavens, with your twinkling grace,
And keep the elves giggling in this merry place!

Wishes Born in Winter's Embrace

In a cozy workshop, elves tap away,
Building bright toys for the big gift day.
They giggle and snicker, share a good joke,
One slips on a block, and it gives him a poke.

With snowflakes falling, the reindeer play,
Prancing around like they're in a ballet.
Santa rolls over in a big fluffy chair,
A cookie stash hidden, beneath his bear stare.

The list is long, but naps are required,
"Twas the night before Christmas," he feels so inspired.
But with every snore, a wish floats out,
Hoping for laughter and a little less doubt.

So gather around, let the merriment grow,
With jingle bells ringing, and cocoa in tow,
For in winter's embrace, joy fills the air,
Santa's chuckles echo, beyond all compare.

Jingle in the Workshop

Elves dance in rhythm, with bells on their toes,
Painting bright gifts, filling sacks with some prose.
One juggles the toys but drops a few cats,
They parade through the room, just like acrobats.

A mischief of trouble brews under the trees,
While Santa keeps chuckling, sipping hot tea.
He leaps in his boots, what a sight to behold,
With candy canes swinging, his heart feels so bold.

Then a reindeer slides in, with a ludicrous grin,
Claiming he's ready to head out and spin.
But he trips on a string, and takes a big dive,
The laughter erupts—oh, how they survive!

With a wink and a nudge, off they all go,
Riding a sleigh in the glittering snow.
The jingle bells jangle, the fun never ends,
In the workshop of wonders, where joy always blends.

The Midnight Sleigh Ride

Beneath the moon's glow, Santa jumps in delight,
A sleigh full of giggles, ready for flight.
Reindeer buck forward, pulling with glee,
Off to the rooftops, as wild as can be.

They zoom past the stars, with a whoosh and a whirl,
Each child asleep, each dream takes a twirl.
With a hearty laugh, Santa lets out a cheer,
"Don't wake up the kids, or it'll ruin the cheer!"

But oh, his belly shakes like a bowl full of jelly,
Through chimneys he slides, albeit a tad smelly.
He dances with joy as he munches a pie,
And no one suspects as he sneaks by the sky.

He slips back in style, his laugh ringing bright,
A jingle of joy marks the magical night.
With wishes bestowed from the heights far above,
Midnight sleigh rides are packed full of love.

Secrets of the North Pole

In the North Pole's corners, where secrets abound,
Whispers of laughter and joy are profound.
Elves share gossip beneath twinkling lights,
While reindeer are plotting their snowy delights.

A naughty elf snags Santa's favorite hat,
Dancing in mischief, it seems he is fat.
Yet Santa just chuckles, knows where it's hidden,
In a box of candy, that's sweetly forbidden.

Hot cocoa erupts with marshmallows galore,
As plans are made up for the big gift store.
"You think we have time for a snowball fight?"
Santa hoists up a snowman, ready for the night.

With secrets unfolding, and giggles that bloom,
They wriggle and wrestle inside of their room.
At the North Pole, fun's just the way that it's spun,
With elves full of laughter, the work's never done.